Kelvin Godwin

Copyright

For more information and questions, contact

kelvin.godwin24@gmail.com

+234(0)808-619-1244

+234(0)903-826-0849

Be Productive, Be Successful, Be the Best you can Be...

Acknowledgement

Special Thanks to my friends and family for their support. We are grateful to subscribers of African Jobs and Elite Business Minds for insights and comments and to those who partake in our survey, Thank you. To employers of labour, employees and job seekers alike, we appreciate you for your kind gestures and thank you for your cooperation. Special appreciation to everyone that has made this publication Successful whose name was not mention here. Also to you, that purchase and read this book, thank you for your patronage. Read and change your status from unemployed to "fully employed". Happy reading

ABOUT THE AUTHOR

Kelvin Godwin is an Inspirational and Multi-gifted speaker and writer, an Entrepreneur and a business Consultant. He addresses issues concerning entrepreneurship, social, personal and thinking development. He is the founder of Elite Business Minds, KP concepts and a supporter of Job Creation Initiatives throughout Africa. He has spent years writing inspirational and life changing motivational books and articles.

He tends to inspire millions of people far and near and in the world at large through his great books and food for thoughts.

His unique and exceptional abilities to connect to the world originate from his passion to tackle challenges facing the society and the world at large.

This book you are about to read addresses issues concerning unemployment, what to do and what not to do when seeking for a job, skills employers are seeking for in prospective employees and how job seekers can possess such skills to become the Desired employees to the Employer. There are also short tips on how to keep your Job, writing CV/Resume, Cover Letters etc.

This book will change your status. Happy reading

He is open to suggestions and feedbacks. For further Enquiries send an email to

kelvin.godwin24@gmail.com

Or call +234(0)808-619-1244

+234(0)903-826-0849

Be Productive, Be Successful, Be the Best you can Be...

Be Productive, Be Successful, Be the Best you can Be...

Be Productive, Be Successful, Be the Best you can Be...

8

Getting Prepared on Your Job Hunt.

Be Productive, Be Successful, Be the Best you can Be...

10

INTRODUCTION

It has been a great privilege for me over the years to mix and mingle with men and women in numerous area of society, from job seekers, to young and emerging entrepreneur to CEO's of some of the largest brands you can think of. The question on everyone's mind is, how can I get my desired Dream "accomplisher(s)"? For job seekers, this term may be "how can I get my desired DREAM JOB" while for CEO's and entrepreneurs, the question is "how can I get the desired employee that will help support my visions and dreams". So in essence, everyone wants something, not just anything but something special and unique to meet a particular need.

So have this at the back of your mind that while you as a Job seeker is seeking, wishing and praying to have "your desired DREAM JOB", the employer(s) are also wishing and seeking for their "desired dream Employee" that will boost the company productivity positively.

This book, " How to Get Your Desired DREAM JOB" is design to help Job seekers develop themselves to be the employees, employers are seeking for and are will do anything to have and keep them ("fight to have"). Imagine your boss or intending employer having much value in you as an asset to have and hold on to while trusting you on the job. That's the dream of every employee; to be in a place where they can grow, and be appreciated for their inputs on the job.

This book is fashion to train and guide you on the necessary skills that are required in the work place. Its aim is to help you develop yourself, on how to get your dream job and also ways to keep the job of your dreams. Trust me when I say that, being out of Job every few months or years is not such a good idea if you want to build a Good career. There are also tips on how to search and find the Job you desire.

Be Productive, Be Successful, Be the Best you can Be...

HOW TO USE THIS BOOK

This book is designed to tackle various aspects of life and the Job market, which Job seekers should concentrate and work on in order to be the much desired and sought after employee employers are seeking for. You can read through for knowledge purpose and equip yourself with the right information pertaining to the Job Market. However, if you are using this book as a tool to get the right Job, I advise that you study each point carefully and take at least five (5) minutes to answer the self discovery questions in section one and also focus on the employers seeks for in chapter two to improve yourself on those skills. The rest part of the book is designed to make you "stand out in the crowd". This book is divided into Six sections. Section One deals with Self Discovery and Mastery; an important concept that all great workers and leaders dwells on. Section Two deals on some of the basic skills employees should possess in order to succeed in any working environment. Section Three is on Job

Market Ethics; things to do and things not to do while seeking for a job. Section Four shows you five simple and practicable ways you can land your dream Job. Section Five is designed to get you prepared on your Job search, CV/Resume writing, Cover Letter Writing and things to know and apply when going for an Interview to get you that desired dream Job. Section Six prepares you on what to do when you already have the Job (Job retain-ability and how to quit a job when the need arises). Read to the end for the total package.

Be Productive, Be Successful, Be the Best you can Be...

Section One

Self discovery

Know thyself - Socrates

1   SELF DISCOVERY AND MASTRY

In life everything that exists has a purpose of its existence. Before one can get hold of a job or work effectively as an employee or control anything that exists around him/her, that individual has to first of all understand HIMSELF. This is what is called Self Concept/Discovery. One the major problem facing the human race is that most people assume that they already know and understand themselves and at such there is no need for them to do any study as regards that. I wish to inform you that if you are among such persons you are wrong.

I was invited as a guest speaker in a Financial Empowerment Summit held in Nigeria, West-Africa and during the course of the Summit, I made mention of Self discovery as one of the first and major skill one has to master before going into

Be Productive, Be Successful, Be the Best you can Be...

any business or job. The audience looked at me with disdain in their faces like I have just mentioned that "Planet Venus is not in existence". By the way, the room was filled with silence and thoughts were running deep through their mind, when I started to clarify them on what self discovery is all about. I asked them a question. The question that is so obvious to all mankind but yet left unanswered. That question is WHO ARE YOU? Some were quick to answer the question of 'who are you' by virtue of their names, place and other physical things that surround them, like residence, ethnicity etc. Then the next question that followed is, "What are You?" for the next 10 minutes nobody was willing to speak, then I pressed on and persuaded them to speak freely; let's just say it won't be nice to reveal the sort of answers I got there, it was terrible. I didn't end there; I asked a third question, **What is Unique about You? Which can also be likened to as "what is your selling Point"?** Still some were

17

moping and others were saying different things which seems ok to them but shows they have not done proper research or study on themselves.

Most times we make the mistakes of trying to study others when we have not of all study ourselves. Before one can be set to control or rule over anything, one must first of all rule over his or herself.

It's not the mountain we conquer, but ourselves –
Edmund Hillary

The concept of self is so important that it cannot be overemphasised. Without it you will not be efficient in your job or anything you do, and you cannot take charge of the things surrounding you. That's why one of my favourite quotes from a great philosopher says: Man Know thy self

Man Know thy self – Socrates

The bible also says that my people perish for lack of knowledge; this knowledge includes who you are in every facet.

To be in top performance in your work, career or to succeed in other endeavours in life, the first place to begin preparation is yourself. Secondly you have to note that you are an asset: not only that, you are an individual that has valuable skills that has market value. What Employers are seeking for is the value prospective employees can bring to the table in their scheme of things and how they can improve the organization for the better. The world of business is 'Values for Value'.

A mastery of yourself: your strengths and weaknesses will enable you approach potential employers with confidence and clearly state what personal set of skills you are bringing to the table that will enhance their operations and profitability.

This section will show you how you can discover yourself by answering various questions that pertains to you.

19

I want you to take at least five (5) minutes to sincerely answer each of these questions.

1.   Who am I

2.   What do I really want in life

3.   What is my vision

4.   What is my purpose

5.   What is/are my Uniqueness

6.   What are my strengths

7.   What are my weaknesses

8.   What are my talents and skills (marketable or hobby.)

1.1   STRENGTHS

Questions you need to answer concerning Strength

1.   Do you have special knowledge in any field or sector in life?

2.   What peculiar skills, talents and abilities do you possess?

3. Who can be of help in areas of advice, support or help you maximize your strength?

4. Does your intelligence preference show strength?

5. What personal behavioural traits do you possess that constitute strength?

6. What supporting resources do you possess that complement your strength?

7. What is already working well for you that will prove useful to the cultivation of your strength?

1.2   Weaknesses

Questions you need to answer concerning Weaknesses

1. What are your limitations or boundaries?

2. What is not working in a particular area in your life right now?

3. What behavioural traits do you have that are weakness in this area?

Be Productive, Be Successful, Be the Best you can Be...

4.   Does your intelligence preference show weakness?

5.   Are there resources that you lack and really needs?

6.   What does FEAR feels like, in your body?

7.   What skills are needed in these areas that you lack?

8.   Do you have low motivation or are you unmotivated?

1.3 Opportunities

Questions you need to answer concerning Opportunities

1.   What opportunities (dreams, wishes, goals) do you wish to make a reality?

2.   Will you be able to take advantage of your strength to pursue these?

3.   Are there any special tools you can use, develop or borrow to help?

4.   Do you have weaknesses that will stop your goals?

5. Does your personality or motivational needs indicate any opportunities that you haven't previously considered?

6. What could you improve in the area of vision or goals that will have most impacts in your life?

7. What major change do you need in your life that will improve you?

1.4   Threats

Questions you need to answer concerning Threats

1. What external threats (changes in income, events, environment etc.) that could affect you negatively?

2. What obstacles are in your way?

3. Do any of your weaknesses increase the level of these threats or its impact?

4. What opportunities are best for you to pursue?

5. What strength do you possess that could help you reduce the identified threats?

Be Productive, Be Successful, Be the Best you can Be...

1.5 Other questions you need to answer include:

❖ **What do people say about me?**

Many people think that people's opinion about them does not count and what others say or feel about them is none of their business, but this has been side tracked by an important document that get you a good position in a good company and that is reference letter. Reference letter shows how important the opinions of others are, to your personal growth and development in field of work and career. In accessing, discovering and developing your potential, skills and competence, people's opinion could be of immense help to you. The mirror (self discovery/personal opinion) is good, but there are certain parts of the human body the mirror cannot reflect. These are spots that others have to bring to your notice for you to work on.

Be Productive, Be Successful, Be the Best you can Be...

❖ **What do I need right now more than anything else?**

"Too often, we neglect what we most need to be happy and healthy," For instance, you might need relaxation or sleep, a massage or an exercise. Whatever it is, respond to your need. Doing so helps you, not only address your short-term needs but also, by extension, your long-term happiness.

❖ **What feeling do I want most in my life? What do I want to be doing more of in my life? What do I want to be doing less of in my life?.**

For instance, "we might want a feeling of peace and relief but keep signing up for high-pressure responsibilities," When we're creating a fulfilling life, it's important to cut out the things that weigh us down and add the things that lift us up.

❖ **What am I resisting, or attaching to?**

For many of us the fear of not being enough or not having something turn out the way we want shows up as resistance or attachment and prevent growth.

However, when you identify what you're resisting or attaching to, you can refocus on cultivating acceptance and expansion.

❖ **What are my gifts? How can I share them with the world?**

For instance, your gifts might include a good sense of humour, playing the piano, acting with kindness, creating art and volunteering your time, managing people, ability to coordinate and organize people etc. You should fine a convenient way to share it with the world. It can be through recorded media or books, or sharing such gift through meaningful work to your employer and the society etc.

❖   **What meaning can I draw from this experience?**

Every experience has a purpose and potential lesson. Of course, the lesson may be tough to swallow, but doing so "prompts awareness, curiosity, compassion, resilience." In other words, focusing on the lesson helps you to keep going in tough times.

❖   **What kind of personality do I have?**

The kind of personality you possess will determine how well you can be able to handle tasks, cope with colleague at work and also build team work.

Be Productive, Be Successful, Be the Best you can Be...

This can be shown in your temperament or temperaments blend. Are you a quiet person or an outgoing person, an introvert or an extrovert? Knowledge of your personality type will help you make certain career decisions that will align with your nature. For more on temperaments and personality read books on them or you can get Tim Lahaye book titled 'Why you act the way you do' or any other books on Temperaments.

Be Productive, Be Successful, Be the Best you can Be...

SECTION TWO

SKILLS EMPLOYERS SEEK FOR IN EMPLOYEES

These are set of skills employers seeks for when employing someone or hiring people to work with them. They include:

1.   Critical and creative thinking/Problem solving Abilities

2.   Thinking Ability

3.   Team work skills

4.   Communication skills

5.   Emotional intelligence

We live in an information age; those who are able to grasp and utilize information will excel better than those who don't – Kelvin Godwin

Be Productive, Be Successful, Be the Best you can Be...

2 PROBLEM SOLVING, CRITICAL AND CREATIVE THINKING

As you begin your job, problems solving and critical or creative thinking are inevitable skills you ought to have or developed. These are the realities you will find in an organization.

Problems can be described as situations that pose a threat to your advancement in whatever tasks you are performing. In life and in the workplace, problems are bound to occur, so there is no need to panic when faced with one. Your method of solving such problem depends on the types of tools and knowledge you utilize.

The ability to solve problems when they arise is a key skill/ability that will help you in your workplace and must be cultivated effectively.

2.1 Here is a three steps Problem solving methodology.

➢ Step one: Identify and define the problem

➢ Step two: the decision making process

➢ Step three: Planning and organising

Problem solving steps.

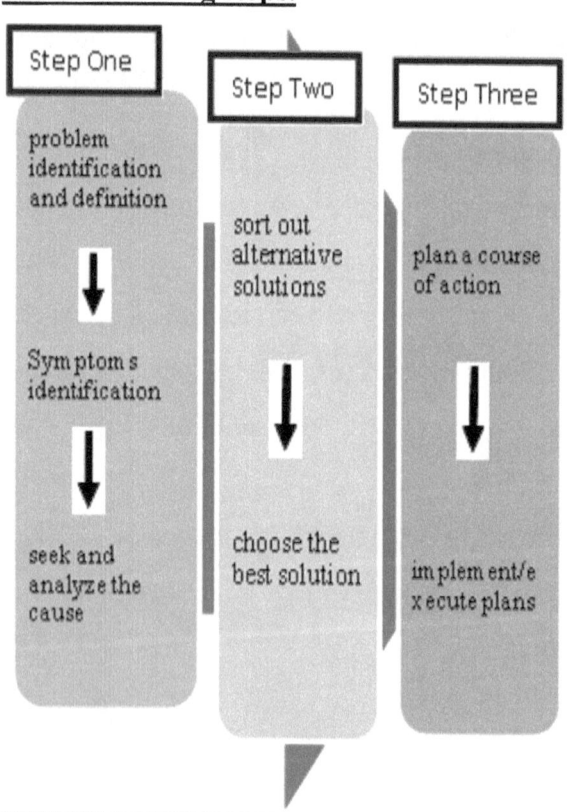

Be Productive, Be Successful, Be the Best you can Be...

➤ **Step one: Identify and define your problem and causes**

a. **Describe the problem**: Being able to describe the problem helps you know how the problem affect your goals and give you clue on how to tackle it or where to begin.

b. **Discover the symptoms**: like diseases that have symptoms, problems also have symptoms. This indicates where it affects or its origin/source. Note that symptoms should not be confused for the real problem.

c. **Seek and analyse the cause**: every problem has a cause; your ability to locate the cause of such problem will aid you in solving it from its roots. The best solution to destroying an unwanted tree is from its roots.

➤ **Step two: Decision making**

a. **Generating alternate solutions**: this is where you come-up with a lot of solutions, adequate solutions that best solve the problem. Here are some tools for generating solutions:

Be Productive, Be Successful, Be the Best you can Be...

1. **Brainstorming**: This is a creative thinking process that generates as many ideas/solutions as possible, within a given time. Allow your ideas to flow free and write whatever comes to mind however silly they are, it might just be the best solution or a clue to the best solution.

2. **Utilize your experience**: after identifying a problem, you might find out that such problem/situations have occurred before as a personal encounter or a close friend of yours has encountered such. All you have to do is use your previous experience to tackle such problem.

3. **Seek solutions from experts**: there is no problem or situation that is totally new, someone somewhere has gone through it and has become a master in solving problems in such field. When you identify the problem and locate the field(s) in which the problem exists. Get experts on such fields towards helping you to come up with a cogent and workable solution. Note that every problem exists within certain field(s) of expertise.

b.   **Evaluation**: once the set of possible solutions have been identified, it is now time to analyse and evaluate each of the solution and pick the "best" one applicable to the problem.

> **Step three: planning and organizing**

This step has to do with implementing those solutions.

Here are questions you need to ask while implementing.

➢ What needs to be done (the solution)?
➢ Who needs to carry it out?
➢ What resources will be required to accomplish it?
➢ How much of these resources will it take?
➢ How much time is needed?

2.2 Here are tips for making good decision

✓ Focus on what is most important

- ✓ Look ahead
- ✓ Look for the good things that can happen
- ✓ Turn big decision into a series of little decision making process (use goals setting to accomplish that).
- ✓ Do not decide until you are ready.
- ✓ Do what you really want.

Be Productive, Be Successful, Be the Best you can Be...

3 THINKING ABILITY

We can't solve problems by using the same kind of thinking that created them – Albert Einstein.

Most times people confuse creative thinking for worrying. The difference between creative thinking and worrying is that worry creates negative imaginary situations that never existed and may never exist, it focus more on the problem without seeking out adequate solutions to deal with the problems, that's if a problem exists. But creative thinking focuses on realistic situations with the aim of analysing the problems with a goal of providing adequate solution to existing problems. Creative/critical thinking seeks out means of providing solutions to already existing problems.

3.1   Problem Solving Ability Using Critical Thinking: Steps to Take.

➢ Identify the problem: the first step is problem identification, this helps you know if a problem truly exists. It helps you know the source and symptoms of the problem. Sometimes when you think through the point (problem identification) thoroughly, you may find out that there is no real problem, just a misunderstanding of concepts and precepts. If there is no problem, that's good, but if there is, proceed to the next step.

➢ Analyse the problem: analysing the problem has to do with looking at the problem from different angles, from a variety of perspectives. By looking at a problem from many angles, sometimes, you can immediately come up with a resolution right away. Ask yourself the following questions sincerely and seek to answer it sincerely with the aim of proffering solutions:

▪ Is there a problem?

▪ Is the problem real or perceived?

Be Productive, Be Successful, Be the Best you can Be...

- Can I solve it alone or do I need help or expert solution on this?

➢   Brainstorm: brainstorming helps you to come-up with several possible solutions. Note that a problem can be solved in many ways. Brainstorm a list of possible solutions and write down anything that comes to mind no matter how silly it may seem. Narrow your list to the best 'fit' solution. Having a variety of options helps you locate the best solutions.

➢   Narrow your list and decide the "best fit solution": go through your list of possible solutions and get the best suitable solution. Take time to determine what will work best for this particular problem, because what works in one situation might not work in another.

➢   Implement and take action immediately: implement your solutions right away. Delay they say is dangerous. Delaying might escalate the problem. Positive action is what creative thinking is all about. *Take positive action against that problem today!*

39

4   TEAMWORK SKILLS

Teamwork is a very essential skill for any Job seeker or anyone that wish to work alongside people or in an organization to achieve a particular goal. Employers value this skill more than anything else. The workplace has come to a point where we have people of diverse background coming together to achieve a common goal and this can only be achieved through teamwork. Team work can be defined as a collaborative effort by members of a team or group to achieve a common goal. It involves relating, respecting, cooperating and contributing positively to the actualization of set goals.

Your ability to be a team player by contributing positively and work effectively with others from diverse background makes you stand out in your workplace and in life. Remember, two good heads are better than one.

Be Productive, Be Successful, Be the Best you can Be...

4.1 Importance of Team Work in the Workplace

❖ **Timely resolution of problems**: When more than one person is working on any given task, problem can be quickly discovered and resolved. This means high quality output and fewer mistakes.

❖ **Timely completion of tasks**: Since work is divided amongst team members, tasks can be completed in a timely and efficient manner.

❖ **Division of work**: With a team, complex work can be divided into simpler ones and shared among team members to carry out.

❖ **Multiple view point and ideas**: With a collection of people from various background and diverse views, different ideas and views will be brought forward and examined when required. This will help bring out the best ideas.

Qualities to possess as a team member

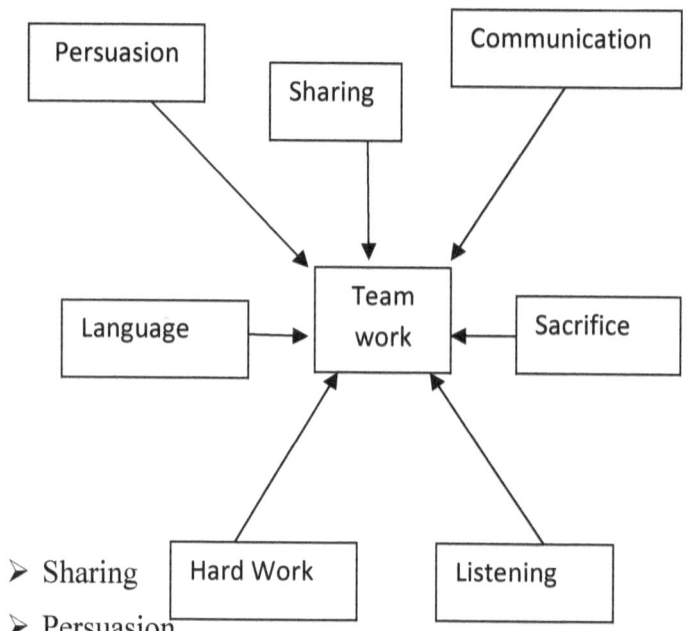

- ➤ Sharing
- ➤ Persuasion
- ➤ Language
- ➤ Listening
- ➤ Hard work
- ➤ Communication
- ➤ sacrifice

Be Productive, Be Successful, Be the Best you can Be...

5 COMMUNICATION SKILLS

Communication is the process of creating, sending and receiving messages that makes sense and is understandable by the parties involve. It is important to note that for communication to be effective, the sender and receiver should be able to understand what is being communicated. Communication comprises of the following:

- ❖ Written
- ❖ Spoken
- ❖ Non-Verbal elements

Every successful leader or workers are good communicators. In communicating, there is a time to speak and there is a time to listen for response or feedback. The ability/learning to listen makes us better learners and helps us in resolving issues faster and better.

5.1   How communication works

This is the structures or channels that make communication possible. It consists of:

❖ The sender or Encoder

❖ The receiver or Decoder

❖ The Message

❖ Feedback

❖ The Medium/Channels

- **The sender or Encoder**: this is the person that starts the communication process by creating and sending out information through a channel or channels to the receiver.

- **The Receiver or Decoder**: he seeks to understands, decodes and interprets the information received.

- **The Message**: this is the communication content that needs to be passed across from the sender to the receiver.

- **Feedback**: this is the response the sender gets from the receiver after the receiver has processed the sender's information/message. The message is proactive while the feedback is reactive.

- **Medium/channels**: this is the medium message passes from the sender to the receiver.

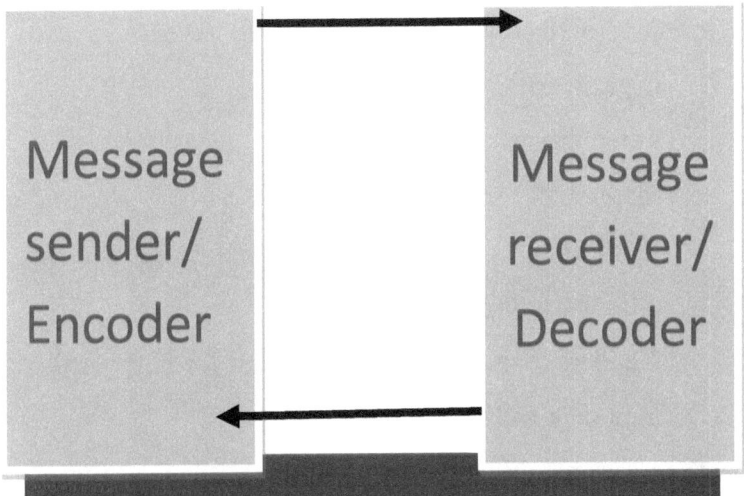

<u>Communication flow diagram</u>

5.2 Medium in which message is communicated

❖   Telephone

❖   Memos

❖   Meetings

❖   Individual conversations

❖   Formal reports

- ❖ Letters
- ❖ Emails
- ❖ Text messages or SMS
- ❖ Or even social media

5.3   Effective communication content and organization

For a message to be effective, it has to possess these qualities:

- ❖ **Audibility**: You should be laud enough for the other party to hear.
- ❖ **Clarity**: it should be clear enough for both parties to understand.
- ❖ **Considerable message length**: a message that is too long may cause people to be bored and too short might not contain the intended message.
- ❖ **Good and understandable language**: Speak in Language that the other parties can understand.
- ❖ **Proper pronunciation**: Pronounce words properly and avoid the use of slangs in a formal Environment.

46

6 EMOTIONAL INTELLIGENCE

6.1 Aristotle's challenge

Anyone can become angry – that is easy. But to be angry with the right person, to the right degree, at the right time, for the right purpose and in the right way – this is not easy – Aristotle

This is the basis of emotional intelligence; it is the ability to control your emotion in every situation. To be able to hold it and release it to the right proportion at the right time to prove the point you wish to express and not to be controlled by your emotions or make irrational decisions in the process.

6.2 Emotional Intelligence (E.I.)

These are non-quantitative skills that govern our interaction with ourselves, other people and our immediate environment. Emotional intelligence is concerned with issues such as understanding our self, others, our relationship with others and our ability to cope with our immediate environment. Emotional quotient **(E.Q)** refers to the level of emotional intelligence (E.I.) an individual posses.

6.3   Five dimensions of Emotional Intelligence.

- ❖ Motivational
- ❖ Social skills
- ❖ Empathy
- ❖ Self awareness
- ❖ Self regulation or self control

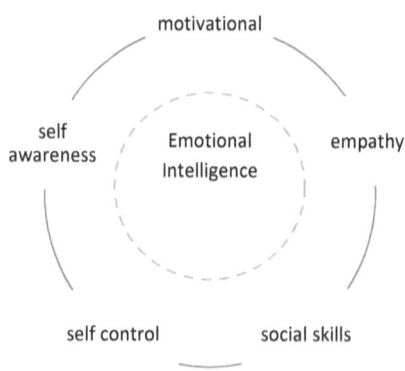

Be Productive, Be Successful, Be the Best you can Be...

Five Dimension of EI

❖ Motivation: motivation is a force that drives a person to do what he or she does. Motivation is of two types; external and internal motivations. People that are highly motivated are driven by internal motivation (internal rewards), such as self satisfaction and personal development other than external rewards, such as money. Internally motivated people are goal getters and they thrive on challenges and challenging situations in other to get outside their comfort zone. They do not need external factors to motivate them.

❖ Social skills: this shows how well you relate or connect with people and form good relationships. It refers to your ability to form close bond with team members or colleagues in order to work easily and share workloads. Those with high social skills can easily   connect   with   people   from   diverse

49

backgrounds and at such; work will be done smoothly and easily.

❖ Empathy: it has to do with understanding other people's emotional make-up so as to be able to tolerate them. Empathy helps you to know when people are just being driven by their emotions and how to tolerate them. With this you are aware of their temperament, moods, feelings and emotions. Your ability to know 'why people act the way they do' and work with them will create a good working environment and increase productivity.

❖ Self Awareness: self awareness is your ability to understand yourself. With self awareness, you understand your moods, feelings, drives and emotions. A high degree of self awareness gives you the ability to understand how your feelings, emotions and moods affect you, other people and your work. It also shows you how to control and manage your emotions.

❖ Self control/regulation: this is the ability to control or regulate destructive and disruptive emotions,

50

feelings and moods. You need to understand that emotions, feelings and moods are created and driven by certain biological chemicals called hormones in our body. While it is true that these hormones are self triggered by our body and there is nothing we can do about that, we can however manage them. This is what self regulation is all about; making decisions based on rational, well thought-out decision, rather than based on emotions, moods and feelings.

For further Enquiries such as getting other information on the relevant skills employers are seeking for, send an email to

kelvin.godwin24@gmail.com   indicating your interest.

Be Productive, Be Successful, Be the Best you can Be...

SECTION THREE

JOB MARKET ETHICS

The future depends on what we do in the present –

Mahatma Gandhi

7 DO'S AND DON'TS OF A JOB SEEKER

We are living in a world of competition, and the job market is no exception to this. Over the years there has been a regular path that has been used by job seekers that have proven and shown successes in getting employment, while other actions or inactions have brought failure to them. The key fact is to know the organization you are going to, research on them and find a cogent way answer questions they wish to ask and appear suited for the job. Remember, the interview is a "likeness concept". If they like your qualification, competence, character and sets of skills you will add to the organization, you are in good shape to be hired.

7.1 The DO's

❖   **It's very important to proofread your Resume and cover letter**.

❖ **Always go through your documents before submitting them**. You can also ask a friend or family member who is knowledgeable in such area to help out in such regards so as to avoid errors or mistakes. Proofread your documents thoroughly to ensure they portray you in good light and pass on the message you intend to communicate to your prospective employers. This is important because your documents represent you and any error to such will be counted against you while you are not there to speak for yourself physically. Documents should be typed using MS-word, use spell-check to correct spellings and grammar errors.

❖ **Keep to Instructions**

When you are applying for a job, you have to obey the rules, regulations or mode of operations (modus operandi) of that organization. There is a reason why they set it that way. Follow the instructions. *There was a written interview conducted by an*

54

organization and as the instruction stated: 'you have less than 15 minutes to these questions. The questions in the question paper were numbering over fifty (50). The next instruction underneath this states that: 'answer question 25 and 40 and close your answer booklet'.

In less than five minutes the examiners started collecting the question paper and answer sheet. They found out that about 93% of the applicants ignored that instruction. What such organisation is looking for is someone who can follow instructions to the latter.

❖   **Make a good first impression**

Before you will be called for interview most likely you will be asked to submit a written application, send CV etc. Make sure your resume and your cover letter is addressed to the specific address on the advert. Qualifications and reason why you are interested in the job should also be stated in your letter. If application is via email, caption the position you are vying for as the subject line, e.g. APPLICATION FOR THE POST OF A FIELD ENGINEER.

Emails/resume should not just be forwarded from an old mail. You should send your application from a fresh "compose" box. Also while sending hard copies of your resume and application use a clean paper and original printouts, don't use photocopies, and package it in a befitting envelope. Using speed post to send your application gives the impression that you are professional. Your first impression builds on your reputation, use it well.

❖ **Know why you are there**

Knowing why you are there gives you an edge in conversation and comporting yourself. Don't apply for a job if you do not have the required qualification and working experience relevant for

Be Productive, Be Successful, Be the Best you can Be...

that job. Jack of all trade master's of none. Before going for an interview you have to first of all do a proper research about the company, the job and the industry. These will help you more in question and answer section of the interview and will show you are interested in what they do. For every employer, it is better to employ someone who loves their company and is enthusiastic about it than someone who is nonchalant about it, or is just there for the pay. Ask reasonable questions if you feel you have to and always listen before you answer or comment on any issue.

❖ Portray your good side

Always portray your good side; dress well, arrive early, plan for your interview, talk confidently, be polite and ask sensible and reasonable questions

Be Productive, Be Successful, Be the Best you can Be...

7.2 THE DON'Ts (Things to Avoid)

☒ Don't give conflicting information

Always make sure all the information and documents you send out in your job applications are consistent in every way such as schools attended and dates, age, work experience etc.

☒ Avoid giving excuses

Ensure you avoid giving excuses when it comes to job interviews. Most job applicants and employees use traffic as one of their major excuse for not resuming early at their duty posts and this doesn't go well with employers. This can be avoided by good timing and proper time management.

☒ Avoid advertising the negative side

Those things that doesn't speak well about you or projects you in a "negative perspective" should be

Be Productive, Be Successful, Be the Best you can Be...

avoided. Things like that can cause you not to be considered for the Job e.g. Religious or Political Views, Personal issues/addictions etc.

.

Be Productive, Be Successful, Be the Best you can Be...

SECTION FOUR

Easy, Simple And Practicable Ways To Get Your Dream Job

The starting point of all achievement is desire. Keep this constantly in mind. Weak desire brings weak results, just as a small fire makes small heat –
Napoleon Hills

Be Productive, Be Successful, Be the Best you can Be...

8 Five Simple and Practicable Ways to Get a Job

In recent times, the job market has been pretty brutal. With so many job seekers vying over the same openings, competition has reached sky-high limits. In response, some candidates are going to crazy lengths to get noticed and are doing all sorts of 'things' to get noticed.

Here are five simple and practicable ways that, when implemented, are sure to make you stand out from your competition and help you land that job offer you have been dreaming of.

8.1. Impress the Employer with Your Resume & Cover Letter

Your resume and cover letter both need to be perfect. This tip sounds like a no-brainer, but you'd be amazed at how many people—qualified, competent people— lose job offers simply because of one 'lazy typo' or what is known as typographical errors. Have a friend or trusted colleague take a look at what you've written. An extra 5 to 10 minutes can make the difference between in securing you an interview and being sent a "thanks, but no thanks" message from HR, so you better work on it.

8.2. Create an Online Profile of yourself

In recent times, hiring managers will likely Google you, so you need an online profile that accurately represents you as a professional—like LinkedIn. Your profile should match your resume, be full of job-specific keywords, and be 100 percent professional. If you are on Facebook or any other social sites platform, It's probably a good idea to delete that picture from your drunken weekend or any other pictures that presents you in the wrong perspective—especially if it's your profile picture.

8.3. Get to Know and connect with the Right People

Getting to know and connect with the right people can be as simple as "knowing someone that knows someone that knows someone who can help out" etc. Getting you to the right job can simply "know the right person". You'd be amazed at how many of your friends and acquaintances will know someone who's looking to hire a candidate with the same skills you have. Plus, they can also put in a good word for you with the hiring manager, which is icing on the cake.

Send out emails to former co-workers, ask around on Facebook, set up lunch meetings with social connections—do whatever it takes to keep your name on other peoples' minds this can be more effective than any other way you can think of.

8.4. Research the Company

It is very important you do a research on the company calling you for an interview. Once you secure an interview, take a moment to let out a sigh of relief and pat yourself on the back. But keep in mind: the hardest part of your job search awaits you.

Answering questions about your previous experience just isn't enough anymore. Before your interview, spend at least one hour researching the company you're hoping to work for. Spend some time on their website. Also research about the position you are applying for, the job description as well as the duties to be carried out in such position if you don't have a clue. Having a

64

few really good questions to ask about the position you are applying for and the company is going to make you shine even brighter than the candidate who's just relying on his or her previous experience. This will surely give you an edge in the interview and in any other conversation relating to such.

8.5. Show Your Appreciation

After an interview, take a few minutes to write a thank-you note. As simple as it sounds, you'd be amazed at how many people pass up this last chance to sell themselves. It's also a great time to ask that really good question that you thought of after the interview was over.

You may see these tips as being obvious and already known to you, you'd be surprised how many of them are overlooked or just simply ignored. Make sure you apply them to your routine and are you're sure to get that desired dream job you've been dreaming about in no time.

To get free interview tips and how to pass any interview, send an email to jobtips7@gmail.com and get this bonus for free instantly.

Be Productive, Be Successful, Be the Best you can Be...

SECTION FIVE

GETTING PREPARED ON YOUR JOB HUNTS

A year from now you may wish you had started today – Karen Lamb

Be Productive, Be Successful, Be the Best you can Be...

9 WRITING AN EFFECTIVE CV/RESUME

In search for your desired job, writing your CV/resume is the very first step to take. Understand that your resume is like a commercial venture where you are the product and your main aim is to draw attention to your work experience and skills. Your resume represents you, and sells your skills and work experience to employers with the hope of considering you suitable for an interview to get the position you are applying for.

9.1   The thirty (30) seconds rule

This rule is all about getting the attention of your prospective/potential employer in 30 seconds or less. This rule is gotten from the average TV commercials that use about 30 seconds or less to get the attention of its audience, so also your resume has about 30 seconds or less to grab the attention of your potential

Be Productive, Be Successful, Be the Best you can Be...

employer. This is because many employers receive large number of resumes and at such; they usually skim over them as quickly as they can. At such your resume should be clearly organised, free from spelling and grammatical errors and easy to read. Ideally it should range from one to three pages with two being the optimum.

9.2   Points to note when designing your resume

❖ It's a summary of your work skills, qualifications, work experiences and accomplishments.

❖ It presents you the opportunity to demonstrate your strengths and focus the reader's attention on those parts you wish to highlights.

❖ Its purpose is to gain potential employer's interest so as to get you an interview.

❖ It speaks on your behalf to prospective employers.

Be Productive, Be Successful, Be the Best you can Be...

9.3   Tips on Resume Writing

✓ Do not crowd your resume. Use short, honest and accurate sentences to describe your work experience. Use bullet to highlight major points.

✓ Use good quality, white A4 size paper for printing your resume.

✓ Use a font type that is easy to read such as Times New Roman or Calibre, with font size of 11 or 12.

✓ Use action verbs to describe your work experience and qualifications.

✓ Don't include salaries or previous salaries or wages you have earned in your resume.

✓ Make sure your resume is directed and tailored to the position you are applying for and at such remove irrelevant work experience.

✓ Only put work experience that best fit the prospective job you are applying for.

✓ Make sure your resume is free from spelling and grammatical errors. Have the resume proofread by a

Be Productive, Be Successful, Be the Best you can Be...

friend, family member or someone who has knowledge of it before submitting it.

9.4   The Dos' and Don'ts of resume writing

The Dos'

☑ Create your own resume.

☑ Create a resume that reflects your career goals positively.

☑ Make sure there are no mistakes of any kind in your resume writing. Have the resume proofread by a friend, family member or someone who has knowledge of it for error detection before submitting it.

☑ Design your resume so that it is logical and easy to read and understand by you and the reader.

☑ Always print your resume on a clean, crisp paper and use a laser jet printer.

☑ Note that the resume may not land you a job, but it can get you an interview for a job.

The Don'ts

☒ Don't send or submit hand written resume (except requested by the employer).

☒ Don't write resume that is too long. Beyond two to three pages. Ideally one or two pages.

☒ Don't send photocopies of your resume to an employer.

☒ Don't include information that will provoke discrimination like:

☒ Religion

☒ Political affiliation

☒ Marital status

☒ Ethnicity

☒ Number and age of children

☒ Age

☒ Gender

☒ Health status

☒ Or Weight

☒ Don't include a photograph of yourself with the resume.

Be Productive, Be Successful, Be the Best you can Be...

SAMPLE OF RESUME

JOHN ROSELINE MARTINS

22 Robert Road, off Azikiwe road, Lagos

John.roseline@gmail.com

0801-111-111-1113

OBJECTIVE: To obtain Physics teaching position in a secondary school with high moral and academic Standards. Utilizing my knowledge and experience to provide quality teaching and knowledge impartation to students, helping them develop their minds and grow positively.

EDUCATION: NNAMDI AZIKIWE UNIVERSITY, Awka, Anambra State.

B.Sc. Physics Education (Second Class Honours)   August 2012

WORK EXPERIENCE:

December 2012-present   VICTORY ACADEMY, Warri, Delta state.

Physics and Chemistry Teacher.

- Resolved class room conflicts.
- Motivate and challenge students through active learning projects and reports.
- Designing of user-friendly reading timetable with students to improve their reading culture.
- Teaching and explaining physics in ways students can easily understand.

ACTIVITIES/PROFESSIONAL MEMBERSHIP

Student Member of Nigeria Physics Society

REFERENCES

Available on request

Be Productive, Be Successful, Be the Best you can Be...

10 WRITING YOUR COVER LETTER

Your cover letter is a way of introducing yourself to the prospective company. It serves as your first contact with a potential employer. It has to be well crafted so as to make a good first impression. It is very important that your cover letter is free from grammatical and spelling errors, and also well organized. This will give a good first impression about you and also give you an edge towards getting an interview. Like the saying goes "first impression matters a lot". Sometimes employers use the cover letter to select applicant they wish to interview.

Note that your cover letters should be well written, organised and neat so that your application will stand a better chance of being considered above several.

Be Productive, Be Successful, Be the Best you can Be...

10.1   Reasons for writing a cover Letter

➢ Some employers estimate how much effort you will put into a job from the way you draft your cover letter.

➢ Some employers use the cover letter to judge how well you express yourself in writing.

➢ Cover letter gives you an opportunity to sell yourself to a potential employer and get invitation for an interview.

➢ Cover letter gives you the opportunity to emphasize the positive aspect of your CV.

10.2   Applicable Tips When Writing your Cover Letter

❖ Use an easy to read font, such as Times New Roman or Calibri. Avoid difficult to read font or stylish font.

❖ Proofread your cover letter and avoid making spelling and grammatical errors.

Be Productive, Be Successful, Be the Best you can Be...

❖ When sending your cover letter, always include your resume.

❖ Let your letter be short and to the point. Sign the letter with a blue or black pen.

❖ Use plain white A4 paper for printing. Make sure the CV and cover letter paper are of the same colour.

❖ Your resume and cover letter should not be hand written. Use a computer to compute them (except stated otherwise).

Be Productive, Be Successful, Be the Best you can Be...

SAMPLE OF COVER LETTER

10 Makro Street,

Ikoyi,

Lagos

4th October 2012

The Chief Executive Officer,

KP Consultant,

32 Ahmadu Bello Way,

Victoria Island,

Lagos.

Dear Sir

APPLICATION FOR THE POST OF HUMAN RESOURCE OFFICER IN YOUR ORGANIZATION

I hereby apply for the post of Human Resource Officer in your organization. I graduated from XYZ University in Industrial Relations with six years of working experience in recruiting, consulting, training, career development, human resources and management. I would be delighted to work in your firm.

My passion for human resource management has intensified over the years. I would be glad if given an opportunity to serve in your organization and help enforce KP Consultant position as a leading firm in the field of Human Resource management.

Please find attached a copy of my resume for your consideration.

Thank you

Yours faithfully,

Ayo Chinedu

Be Productive, Be Successful, Be the Best you can Be...

11   THE INTERVIEW

This is the stage where the employer contacts the applicant, in order to get to know more about his or her skills and personality and how they can fit into his organization if hired. If your search has proceeded to this stage, then we can assume the following:

❖   Your job search found an opening

❖   The interviewers probably have a good perception about you.

❖   Your cover letter and resume were good enough to get you an interview invitation.

At this stage it is all based on how you perform on the interview.

Be Productive, Be Successful, Be the Best you can Be...

11.1   The Different Types of Interview

Companies use different types of interview system to screen potential employees and there is a possibility that you will come across one or more of these in the course of your job search. Put it at the back of mind that you may likely face one or more of these (multiple interviews), depending on the size of the company. Always do backgrounds research about the company as much as you can, and try to find out who will be interviewing you or the hired contracting firm that is in charge of recruitment.

a.   **Committee/panel Interview**:

▪ Here you have more than one interviewer, usually a committee setup for it or a panel.

▪ The panel may consist of three or more interviewers. This gives you a chance to show your group presentation skills.

- Study the personality type of each of the interviewers as quickly as possible and find a way to connect with each of them.

- Maintain good eye contacts with the interviewer who asked you the question but don't ignore the others. Answer each question as calmly as possible and do not rush the answers. Try engaging each one of them through eye contacts.

- Some people are afraid to stand before panel and at such they panic. I want to let you know that the panel is not setup to humiliate or belittle you. What they are there to do is to get the right candidate that will do an effective job with their company, so be calm and bold. Timidity and shyness are amongst traits that employers don't want to see in their organization or in prospective employee, so be bold and sell yourself like you ought to.

b.   Face to Face Interview

- This is the most common type of interview. It is a one-on-one interaction with potential employer.

- Be focus on the person asking you questions. Listen and respond once a question has been asked. Make sure you maintain good eye contact.

- Sell yourself and your skill to the employer when the opportunity presents itself.

- The goal is to establish rapport with the interviewer and show him that your skills and potentials will benefit the organization positively.

c.   Behavioural interview

- In this interview the focus is on asking questions about your past behaviours, which will be use as an indicator to know your future behaviour.

- Behavioural interview questions usually begin with phrases such as "tell me about a time when..." or "give me an example of..." This kind of interview is result oriented. This means that

81

when a question is asked by an interviewer, he is looking for an outcome and your role in achieving that outcome.

d.   Telephone Interview

- This is common these days unlike in the 90's. So prepare yourself for it

- Treat this interview as you would a Face-to-Face interview. Get a quiet space and time to schedule the conversation.

- Listen to the questions carefully before answering. Focus on the conversation and be audible enough so that the interviewer can hear you.

- Have a copy of your resume nearby to serve as reference.

- Whenever you have a telephone interview, if you are using a mobile device, make sure the battery is fully charged and everything is in order for smooth conversation to take place.

e. Case Interview

- Case interview focuses on your problem solving skills. The interviewer will present you with a problem scenario and ask you to apply your knowledge and skills to solve it.

- What the interviewer is looking for is how you can formulate a plan that deals with the problem, sometimes spontaneously. Note that you do not need to come-up with "the ultimate solution" to the problem, your ideas is what is needed and judged.

- Walk your interviewer through the plan step-by-step. It shows that you are methodical and well organized.

- Don't be afraid to ask your interviewer questions when you need clarification. It shows you are inquisitive, proactive and interested.

Be Productive, Be Successful, Be the Best you can Be...

11.2   The interview: Items to carry along

The following are things to bring along when going for an interview

✓   Extra copies of your resume. Always go with at least three copies of your resume. This is because you may be interviewed by more than one person and they might need personal copies.

✓   Go with extra copies of your reference page.

✓   Pen and note pad. Go with writing pad and a pen to write or jot something down. It's a nice idea to be ready to write notes during the interview session for future reference, and also, you can use the note to write down sensible and important questions you may have for the interviewer(s). Asking questions shows that you are attentive and an active listener. Also make sure that you don't look carried away by your writing during the interview.

11.3 Dressing for an interview.

The ground rule is to dress the way you want to be address. Your physical appearance plays an important role in how employers assess your suitability to the firm. The way you dress for an interview speaks a lot about the kind of person you are. Have the following in mind when dressing for an interview:

✓   Have a clean and neat appearance. Make sure all cloths are washed clean and pressed properly. Also make sure your shoes are polished.

✓   For the ladies, avoid wearing heavy makeup and excessive jewellery.

✓   Put on business or professional attire.

❖   Male: clean, neatly pressed collar shirt, trouser, polished shoes, suit is also very good. You may also decide not to wear a tie, but its good you have wear one, depending on the job title or company culture.

❖ Female: clean, neatly ironed top and either a skirt or trouser with polished shoes. Dressing should be

85

formal and well presentable. If you are wearing heels, avoid tall heels.

✓ Maintain good hygiene by making sure you clean and trim your nails, brush your teeth and keep well groomed hair, beard or moustache.

11.4   Interview Tips

✓ Do not chew gum during the interview.

✓ Try to maintain good eye contact with your interviewer(s), but don't stare hard on them.

✓ Shake hands firmly but not an extremely uncomfortable grip. Weak hand shake usually give an impression of lack of confidence and shyness, these traits are not needed in a competitive environment.

✓ Never leave an interview panel without asking a sensible question as it could indicate lack of interest.

✓ Ensure you find out exactly where the venue for the interview is, and how long it would take for you to get there. Avoid lateness; traffic is not a good enough excuse. When it is rainy or in rainy season, you can use an umbrella.

✓ Make sure your phone is switch off or put in silent mode, not vibration. Vibration mode may sometimes make noise that can startle you and may alert the interviewer that your phone is on.

✓ Have a good rapport with all the staff of the company you come across, as the interview is not limited to when you are seated before a panel. You never can tell a person's position in the company or who will put in a word for or against you in the organization.

✓ Carry along extra copies of similar resume to the interview. Also carry photocopies of your credentials and required documents.

✓ In a situation where you forgot to switch off your phone and it rings, switch it off immediately and apologise sincerely.

✓ Avoid the usage of slangs and saying things like "emm", "as if", "you know", "uhh" etc. Keep your use of language strictly formal, and always remember that you are in a formal setting.

✓ Maintain an open attitude

✓ Wait until you are offered a chair before sitting. Also avoid sitting in an extremely relaxed position, as if you are in your living room.

✓ Focus on what value you can add to the organization. Talk at length about what you can do for the company rather than what the company can or should do for you. Questions about salaries or other benefits should not be discussed at this stage until you are offered the job or if it is requested by the interviewer.

✓ Be prepared.

✓ Remember that you are in a formal environment so keep it formal.

✓ Show prospective employer what you can do for them.

✓ Seize the opportunity to sell yourself.

✓ Try to ask sensible questions as the interview progresses.

Be Productive, Be Successful, Be the Best you can Be...

11.5   Potential interview questions and guides to answering them.

It's very important to prepare for potential interview questions as this will get your mind prepared for questions that may come up during the interview. Am sure you don't want to find yourself in "wonderland" while trying to answer questions asked by interviewers. Below is a list of commonly asked questions by interviewers.

➤   Tell me about yourself? This question usually comes first. The best answer is for you to highlight what set you apart from being average in a positive sense. Talk about your school, previous accomplishments and work experience.

➤   What was the biggest success you have had at your last job? What are the biggest failures you have had at your last job? The best applicants are the ones who will admit that they have made a mistake and learn from that mistake. Be honest and speak of how such mistake has made you

89

grow positively. This is an incredible and important trait to any company. If you have not made a mistake, say the truth.

➢ Tell me about the most difficult task/challenge you ever faced? This is to assert if you have faced difficult challenges in the past and how it has affected you. Speak about it with sincerity and how you were able to cope and handle such challenge.

➢ Tell me about your dream job? Do not indicate any specific job or say this current job you are applying for. Instead, stick to specific traits, aspects or fields of what would be your dream job.

➢ Do you have any question about this job? Always prepare questions you will like to ask the interviewer about the company or the position you are being interviewed for, it's a sign that are interested in the position. Have a few questions already in mind when you are going to an

Be Productive, Be Successful, Be the Best you can Be...

interview. Just make sure your questions are intelligent and sensible.

➤ Are you applying for other job? The best way to answer this is to say 'yes, in much the same way you are interviewing other people. We are both trying to find the best fit for what we need and what we want'. Say it in a polite way. But if your answer is truly No, then say so.

➤ What did you learn from your last position? To answer this question, list some technical and non-technical skills you learn or gain from your pervious job. Do not say or insinuate that you did not learn anything from your previous job. This question is asked to know if you are a good learner and if you pay attention to your job.

➤ Have you ever been asked to leave a position? If yes, tell the truth about the experience, be honest when answering this question. If your answer is 'yes', try to find a way to present it as a positive experience. You can use this opportunity to make them know

Be Productive, Be Successful, Be the Best you can Be...

that you have made mistakes in the past and that you have learnt from it.

➢ What are your greatest strength and weakness? Some people usually see such questions as the most difficult questions to answer during an interview. Actually people who can answer such questions are those who know themselves (self discovery). It requires you having the knowledge of "who you are", "your values", "your uniqueness and your goals". You should study the self discovery chapter of this book (chapter one) to know more about yourself. You can also ask your friends to help you out by asking them questions about yourself.

➢ Where do you see yourself in your career five years from now? What are your long term goals? This question tells if you are a long term thinker or not. Long term planners and thinkers are usually in a good, mature mental state and mindset. It indicates great work strength, focus and proactive abilities.

➢ Explain the gap in your work history? If there is a gap in your work history, an employer may want to

Be Productive, Be Successful, Be the Best you can Be...

know why. Be honest and tell them the reason for the gap.

➤ Do you prefer working alone or working with others? From this question the interviewer seek to understand your style of work and your ability to be a team player (work in groups). To answer this, be honest and know that if the position you are applying for requires heavy interaction with other people and your preference is working alone, you will not be able to function effectively in such position.

➤ What did you know about the company? Always do your research about a company before going for an interview. Find out what its operations are, the department you may likely be stationed etc. This shows readiness and that you understand the company.

➤ Why are you interested in the position? This question is tricky; come up with a few things that intrigue you about the company, the position and

93

mention reasons why they interest you and how you can function effectively in such position.

➢ What set you apart from other applicants? This is an opportunity to sell yourself. Bring out those things that are unique about you and how you can use it to improve the company's output positively.

➢ What do you see as the important future trends in this area? Questions like this usually come up when you are being interviewed for a technical or leadership positions. To answer this, you have to prepare well for the interview and make sure you are current with relevant information on such topic by reading magazines, newspapers, articles and other relevant source that contains information pertaining to the job.

11.6 After Interview Follow-Up

The follow-up letter: after the interview session, it's not a bad idea to send a letter or email to the interviewers saying thank you. This gives you a chance to redeem yourself on any question you feel you did badly on, and further reinforce your position in the job.

FOLLOW-UP LETTER

10 Makro Street,

Ikoyi,

Lagos

12th November 2012

Ms. Adam Brian,

Personnel Manager,

Queens Innovations Ltd,

123 Ahmadu Bello Way,

Victoria Island,

Lagos

Dear Ms. Adam,

Thank you for making out time to interview me on Wednesday, November 7, 2012.

It was a pleasure meeting you and your team.

I am enthusiastic about the career opportunity Queens Innovations Ltd offers and the value I can add to your organization that will enhance its operations and productivity. Thank you for your hospitality.

I look forward to your decision.

Sincerely,

Akpan Chris

Enclosure

To get more interview tips and how to pass any interview for free, send an email to jobtips7@gmail.com and get this bonus for free instantly.

SECTION SIX

WHAT TO DO WHEN YOU ALREADY HAVE A JOB

Job Retainability: how to keep your Job

Quitting your Job: here is how to do it right

Accept responsibility for your life. Know that it is you who will get where you want to go, no one else – Les Brown

97
Be Productive, Be Successful, Be the Best you can Be...

12 JOB RETAINABILITY: HOW TO KEEP YOUR JOB

This chapter tells you of things to that will keep you on the Job and make you thrive in it. Many people who land themselves a dream Job after a long search sometimes get kicked out of the job because they couldn't perform very well or they break some rules. Here we will give you "few tips" on guide to success at work.

12.1 GUIDES TO SUCCESS AT WORK

You need to understand about ethics at work, things that will build trust and harmony in a work place.

12.2 Ethics at Work

Ethics are the principles or standards that govern our actions. Ethical behaviour at work can be summarized as honesty, accountability and respect.

Here are some reminders of the practical applications of ethics.

➤ **Accountability**

- Taking responsibility for and "owning" your actions and mistakes
- Avoiding making excuses or blaming others.
- Admitting to "not knowing", and then finding out, to avoid making mistakes.

➤ **Honesty**

- Avoiding "time theft" by being on time, keeping personal tasks out of the workplace and by committing to a full day's work.

- Being truthful.

- Not assuming personal use of workplace equipment or taking work supplies home.

➤ **Making Ethical Decisions**

If you are unsure about the ethics of a situation it may help to ask yourself these questions:

- Is it legal?

- Is it fair?

- How does it make you feel?

- What if your actions were made public?

- Will it harm anyone?

100

- Would you feel differently if it were your business? If you were the customer?

> **Respect in the workplace**

- Respect for self: a healthy lifestyle, optimism and confidence.

- Respect for others: positive work relationships, based on effective communication and appropriate behaviour.

- Respect for the organization: taking an interest in the work being done, and caring for the workplace.

Be Productive, Be Successful, Be the Best you can Be...

13 QUITTING YOUR JOB, HERE IS THE RIGHT WAY TO DO IT

This chapter is important because it will guide you on how go quit a job, when the need arises.

13.1   Job Resignation

In your working career, you might want to quit a job for one reason or the other; be it personal reasons, like family issues or professional ones like advancing to another company. Whatever reason you have, the baseline is this that you have to do it the right way. You have to make sure you leave on a good note and keep the good working relationship you have with your 'soon to be ex-boss', rather than leaving on a bad note or leaving a bad impression. In future you might need their assistance in terms of reference letter or other materials.

13.2   Steps to take when you have made the decision to leave

1. Inform the human resource department or your supervisor.

2. Be truthful as regard your reason for leaving the company.

3. Make sure you give your current employer notice before you leave. Try to review any employment contract and document to see the conditions on the termination of your present employment if you have signed any.

4. Prepare and submit a letter of resignation to the appropriate personnel.

Be Productive, Be Successful, Be the Best you can Be...

LETTER FORMAT WHEN QUITTING A JOB

14 Wose Street

Surulere

Lagos

December 15, 2014

Ms. Adam Brian

Personnel Manager

Queens Innovation Ltd

123 Ahmadu Bello Way

Victoria Island

Lagos

Dear Adams:

It is with regret that I write to inform you of my intention to resign from my position as an assistant manager in QPR Ltd. This is because I have been offered a job as a Manager in XZY Solutions Ltd.

I will resume my new position on January 19, 2015, hence my resignation will take effect on January 15, 2015.

For me, working in QPR Ltd has been a very rewarding experience. I have learned a lot from my colleague and other member of staff. I deeply appreciate the opportunity given to me to work in this organization and look forward to being a good ambassador of this company (QPR Ltd.).

Thank You

Yours faithfully,

Akeem Prince

Be Productive, Be Successful, Be the Best you can Be...

EPILOGUE

We have come to the end of this publication, all that is required from you is to take action and act fast. Time waits for no one. Use this information to improve your life and that of the people living close to you by putting yourself and CV out there for employers to See and consider. There are lots of Jobs out there for those who possess the required skills employers are looking for and you are one of such.

Note: if your immediate qualification is not getting you a job, then there is need to improve and build on it by doing other relevant CERTIFIED COURSES that are in high demand by employers to put you on the spot light.

I will like to hear and read your story on how this book was able to cause a meaningful input to you getting a Job. Send us an email or call us on the contacts given below.

105

For further Enquiries such as getting other relevant information on GETTING YOUR DESIRED DREAM JOB, past and future publications by the Author on this topic send us an email on

kelvin.godwin24@gmail.com

Or call +234(0)808-619-1244

+234(0)903-826-0849

Be Productive, be successful, be the best you can be...

Be Productive, Be Successful, Be the Best you can Be...